Merry Moments: A Collection of Christmas Poems

Dan Ashford

Published by Bright Minds Books, 2024.

While every precaution has been taken in the preparation of this book, the publisher assumes no responsibility for errors or omissions, or for damages resulting from the use of the information contained herein.

MERRY MOMENTS: A COLLECTION OF CHRISTMAS POEMS

First edition. December 3, 2024.

Copyright © 2024 Dan Ashford.

ISBN: 979-8230656999

Written by Dan Ashford.

Table of Contents

Poem 1: "The Christmas Tree" 1
Poem 2: "Baking Cookies" 2
Poem 3: "Wrapping Gifts" 3
Poem 4: "The Christmas Stocking" 4
Poem 5: "Sleigh Ride Adventure" 5
Poem 6: "Caroling in the Snow" 6
Poem 7: "A Snowman's Dream" 7
Poem 8: "Santa's Workshop" 8
Poem 9: "The Christmas Feast" 9
Poem 10: "The Christmas Wreath" 10
Poem 11: "The Christmas Parade" 11
Poem 12: "Reindeer Games" 12
Poem 13: "The Christmas Eve Night" 13
Poem 14: "Gingerbread House" 14
Poem 15: "The Nativity Scene" 15
Poem 16: "The Snowflakes Fall" 16
Poem 17: "The Christmas Tree" 17
Poem 18: "The Gift of Giving" 18
Poem 19: "The Christmas Angel" 19
Poem 20: "The Snowy Morning" 20
Poem 21: "Santa's Workshop" 21
Poem 22: "The Christmas Star" 22
Poem 23: "The Christmas Eve Wish" 23
Poem 24: "The Christmas Carol" 24
Poem 25: "The Christmas Lights" 25
Poem 26: "The Christmas Snowman" 26
Poem 27: "The Christmas Cookie" 27
Poem 28: "The Christmas Stockings" 28
Poem 29: "The Christmas Countdown" 29
Poem 30: "The Gingerbread House" 30
Poem 31: "The Christmas Parade" 31

Poem 32: "The Christmas Wish List" 32
Poem 33: "The Christmas Tree Farm" 33
Poem 34: "The Christmas Eve Bell" 34
Poem 35: "The Christmas Morning" 35
Poem 36: "The North Pole" 36
Poem 37: "The Snowflake Dance" 37
Poem 38: "The Christmas Wreath" 38
Poem 39: "The Christmas Fire" 39
Poem 40: "The Christmas Angels" 40
Poem 41: "The Christmas Cookie Jar" 41
Poem 42: "The Christmas Market" 42
Poem 43: "The Christmas Stocking Surprise" 43
Poem 44: "The Christmas Carolers" 44
Poem 45: "The Snowman's Hat" 45
Poem 46: "The Christmas Lights" 46
Poem 47: "The Christmas Countdown" 47
Poem 48: "The Christmas Snowball" 48
Poem 49: "The Christmas Carol" 49
Poem 50: "The Christmas Eve Sky" 50
Poem 51: "The Christmas Letter" 51
Poem 52: "The Christmas Tree Lights" 52
Poem 53: "The Gingerbread House" 53
Poem 54: "The Christmas Parade" 54
Poem 55: "The Christmas Countdown Calendar" 55
Poem 56: "The Christmas Choir" 56
Poem 57: "The Christmas Story" 57
Poem 58: "The Christmas Carrot" 58
Poem 59: "The Christmas Bells" 59
Poem 60: "The Christmas Sleigh" 60
Poem 61: "The Christmas Stockings" 61
Poem 62: "The Christmas Snowflakes" 62
Poem 63: "The Christmas Cookies" 63
Poem 64: "The Christmas Magic" 64

Poem 65: "The Christmas Wreath" 65
Poem 66: "The Christmas Angels" 66
Poem 67: "The Christmas Star" 67
Poem 68: "The Christmas Poinsettia" 68
Poem 69: "The Christmas Wish" 69
Poem 70: "The Snowman's Hat" 70
Poem 71: "The Christmas Ribbon" 71
Poem 72: "The Christmas Tree Ornaments" 72
Poem 73: "The Christmas Train" 73
Poem 74: "The Christmas Carolers" 74
Poem 75: "The Christmas Angel" 75
Poem 76: "The Christmas Gifts" 76
Poem 77: "The Christmas Morning" 77
Poem 78: "The Christmas Magic of Giving" 78
Poem 79: "The Christmas Cookie Jar" 79
Poem 80: "The Christmas Village" 80
Poem 81: "The Christmas Parade" 81
Poem 82: "The Christmas Sleigh" 82
Poem 83: "The Christmas Bells" 83
Poem 84: "The Christmas Carol" 84
Poem 85: "The Christmas Lantern" 85
Poem 86: "The Christmas Wreath" 86
Poem 87: "The Christmas Snowflake" 87
Poem 88: "The Christmas Stocking" 88
Poem 89: "The Christmas Pudding" 89
Poem 90: "The Christmas Lights" 90
Poem 91: "The Christmas Lullaby" 91
Poem 92: "The Christmas Angel's Message" 92
Poem 93: "The Christmas Tree Lights" 93
Poem 94: "The Christmas Joy in Our Hearts" 94
Poem 95: "The Christmas Eve Stars" 95
Poem 96: "The Christmas Story" 96
Poem 97: "The Christmas Angels" 97

Poem 98: "The Christmas Morning" 98
Poem 99: "The Christmas Wish" 99
Poem 100: "The Spirit of Christmas" 100

Description

"Merry Moments: A Collection of Christmas Poems" is a heartwarming collection of 100 festive poems that capture the magic of the holiday season.

From twinkling Christmas lights to the joy of gift-giving, each poem brings to life the simple yet profound moments of Christmas with warmth and cheer. Perfect for families and young readers, this book invites you to celebrate the spirit of love, kindness, and togetherness.

Whether you're baking cookies, hanging stockings, or singing carols, this collection will fill your heart with the joy of Christmas and create lasting memories for all.

Dedication

This book is dedicated to all those who hold Christmas in their hearts, to those who share the joy of the season with laughter, kindness, and love.

To the families who come together to celebrate, to the children whose faces light up with wonder at each new Christmas tradition, and to those who cherish the magic of the holiday season—this collection is for you.

May these poems inspire warmth in your home, bring joy to your heart, and remind you of the beauty of the simple, merry moments that make Christmas unforgettable.

Preface

"Merry Moments: A Collection of Christmas Poems" was created to capture the special, fleeting moments that make Christmas so meaningful. The holiday season has a unique way of bringing people together—whether it's the twinkling lights, the aroma of freshly baked cookies, or the joy of gift-giving. Each poem in this collection reflects the pure, unadulterated joy of those simple yet magical moments that are often shared with loved ones.

Christmas is a time for tradition, joy, and reflection, and this book aims to celebrate all the things that make it so special. From snowflakes to Santa, from Christmas trees to stockings hung with care, these poems embody the warmth, love, and spirit of the holiday season.

I hope that as you read these poems, you feel a renewed sense of Christmas wonder, no matter your age. May these verses bring smiles, warmth, and cherished memories to your holiday celebrations.

Poem 1: "The Christmas Tree"

The tree stands tall with twinkling lights,
A beacon in the snowy nights.
Each ornament a story told,
Of Christmases, both new and old.
The smell of pine fills up the air,
With joy and love, we all prepare.
The star upon the highest bough,
Glows gently like a sacred vow.
The presents stacked beneath its shade,
Of sparkling paper, ribbons laid.
We wait with hope, so full of cheer,
For Christmas morning to appear.
The children sing their carols bright,
As snowflakes fall, a pure delight.
The warmth of fire flickers low,
While all around the cold winds blow.
The tree's soft glow shines far and wide,
A symbol of the season's pride.
With family gathered near and dear,
We cherish all the love we share.
And as the night turns still and deep,
The world seems calm, as all things sleep.
The Christmas tree stands proud and true,
A gift of joy, for me and you.

Poem 2: "Baking Cookies"

The kitchen fills with flour's dust,
As Christmas time is here, we trust.
We roll the dough and cut the shapes,
Of stars and trees, and snowy flakes.
The oven hums with warmth and cheer,
As cookies bake, we all draw near.
The scent of sweetness fills the air,
A holiday joy beyond compare.
We sprinkle sugar, oh so light,
On gingerbread men, a tasty sight.
With icing swirls, so bright and bold,
Each cookie's story now unfolds.
The timer dings, and out they come,
A golden hue, they make us hum.
We stack them high, a festive treat,
So perfect for the Christmas feast.
With sprinkles, chocolate chips, and cream,
The cookies shine, like a dream.
We share them with our friends and kin,
A sweet tradition to begin.
And as we munch on cookie bliss,
We share a merry, heartfelt kiss.
For Christmas time is here to stay,
And love is baked in every way.

Poem 3: "Wrapping Gifts"

The paper crinkles, ribbon curls,
Each present wrapped for boys and girls.
With care and love, the packages shine,
A gift to say, "You're truly mine."
The tape is sticky, the scissors sharp,
We cut and fold with joy to spark.
Each box and bag, a secret kept,
Until the Christmas morning's step.
We tie the bows with perfect hands,
As paper wraps like snowy sands.
The colors bright, the textures sweet,
A perfect wrapping, quite complete.
The names are written on the tags,
For every gift, each one it brags.
With laughter loud, we wrap and twine,
And make each gift look so divine.
The stack grows high, the pile so grand,
Of ribbons, gifts, both neat and planned.
We smile with joy, hearts all aglow,
As Christmas Day begins to show.
The gifts are waiting, ready, bright,
To be unwrapped on Christmas night.
And though the presents will soon be seen,
The love inside will always gleam.

Poem 4: "The Christmas Stocking"

We hang our stockings by the fire,
Each one adorned with bright desire.
With hopes and dreams, we wait to see,
What gifts await beneath the tree.
The cozy room begins to glow,
As flames in the fireplace softly flow.
We giggle and chat, our hearts are light,
Anticipating the Christmas night.
The stockings sway in festive cheer,
Each one a promise drawing near.
What treats will fill them, what surprise,
A tiny treasure in disguise.
The candy canes, the little toys,
All wrapped with love for girls and boys.
We hang them high with joyful hands,
And smile at all the holiday plans.
The magic stirs, the night is near,
A sense of wonder, calm and clear.
Our stockings wait, so soft and wide,
With hopes of Christmas wrapped inside.
And when the morning sun does rise,
We'll see the gifts before our eyes.
The stockings, filled with love and glee,
A symbol of our family.

Poem 5: "Sleigh Ride Adventure"

The sleigh bells jingle in the air,
As snowflakes twirl without a care.
We bundle up and snuggle tight,
For a sleigh ride in the silent night.
The horse's hooves make music clear,
As we glide through winter's cheer.
The chilly air, the frosty breeze,
Whispers secrets through the trees.
The sky above is dark and deep,
As winter's beauty makes us leap.
Through snowy fields we race with glee,
As free as any bird might be.
The moonlight dances on the snow,
While stars above begin to glow.
The sleigh ride takes us far and wide,
Across the world with Christmas pride.
We laugh and shout and sip hot cocoa,
As the night becomes a winter show.
The sleigh ride's journey, full of grace,
Leaves joy and peace in every place.
And as the ride comes to a close,
The warmth of home begins to grow.
We thank the stars, we thank the night,
For this sleigh ride of pure delight.

Poem 6: "Caroling in the Snow"

We gather 'round, our voices rise,
Caroling beneath the snowy skies.
With every word, with every cheer,
We spread the warmth of Christmas near.
The cold wind blows, but we're all bright,
Our songs like stars, a shining light.
We walk through streets of snow and gleam,
A winter's magic, like a dream.
The chimneys puff with smoke and cheer,
As we sing louder, far and near.
The doorbells ring, the neighbors smile,
As Christmas joy spreads mile by mile.
The melody is soft and sweet,
A caroler's heart begins to beat.
The words we sing are full of grace,
A smile on every friendly face.
Through frosty windows, lights aglow,
We watch the Christmas wonders show.
The world feels small, the night feels wide,
As carolers walk with hearts open wide.
And as we sing our final song,
The spirit of Christmas lingers long.
The snow keeps falling, soft and bright,
While joy fills every heart tonight.

Poem 7: "A Snowman's Dream"

A snowman stands, so tall and grand,
With buttons bright and mittened hand.
His coal-black eyes, a smile so wide,
He guards the yard with snowy pride.
The snow falls gently all around,
As whispers of the winter sound.
The snowman dreams of snowflakes new,
Of frosty mornings, bright and true.
He dreams of playing with the kids,
And riding sleighs through snowy grids.
Of snowball fights and snowman friends,
His joy and laughter never ends.
His scarf is red, his nose is bright,
He stands there proud in moonlit light.
But in his heart, he holds a wish,
To dance beneath the stars so swish.
As night falls soft, the stars appear,
The snowman dreams of joy and cheer.
Of snowflakes twirling in the sky,
As winter whispers, passing by.
And though he's made of ice and snow,
He'll watch the world as seasons go.
For in his dream, so deep and wide,
He'll live in hearts, with love as guide.

Poem 8: "Santa's Workshop"

In Santa's shop, the elves do toil,
Their hands all busy with the soil.
They craft the toys with special care,
For children everywhere to share.
The hammers tap, the machines hum,
As gifts are made and dreams are spun.
The elves wear smiles, their eyes all bright,
Their Christmas cheer a wondrous sight.
From dolls to trains, from bikes to sleds,
Each gift is made with happy threads.
The toys come to life with a little cheer,
As Santa's magic draws them near.
The sparkle in their eyes so pure,
As elves work fast, their hearts secure.
The gift of giving fills the air,
A joy that's meant for all to share.
In Santa's shop, there's never night,
The work is done with love and light.
The elves, with hearts so full and true,
Make every Christmas dream come true.
So when you wake on Christmas day,
Remember the elves and what they say—
With love and joy, and hands so skilled,
Santa's magic will be fulfilled.

Poem 9: "The Christmas Feast"

The table's set, the candles glow,
The Christmas feast begins to show.
With turkey, ham, and pies so sweet,
A meal for all, a festive treat.
The mashed potatoes, soft and warm,
The cranberry sauce, a joyful swarm.
The veggies fresh, the stuffing right,
A Christmas dinner, pure delight.
The family gathers 'round the table,
With smiles and stories, all so stable.
We pass the food, the laughter flows,
As Christmas cheer and joy bestows.
The plates are full, the cups are raised,
We share the joy of days long praised.
Each bite a gift, each toast a song,
We celebrate all we've known so long.
With laughter loud and voices bright,
We savor each delicious bite.
For Christmas isn't just the meal,
It's sharing love, the joy we feel.
And when the dinner's finally done,
We know that Christmas has just begun.
The feast was sweet, but in our hearts,
The love of Christmas never parts.

Poem 10: "The Christmas Wreath"

A wreath of holly, green and bright,
Hangs on the door with Christmas light.
Its red berries shine, so pure and true,
A welcome sign for me and you.
The twigs are woven, round and wide,
A circle of love with Christmas pride.
The bow is tied with perfect care,
A symbol of the joy we share.
The winter winds may howl and blow,
But inside, warmth begins to glow.
The wreath a sign of love and cheer,
That Christmas time is drawing near.
Each holly leaf, each berry red,
Tells stories of the joy we've spread.
With every twig, so soft and green,
A peaceful Christmas scene is seen.
The wreath is hung, the door is bright,
A beacon in the quiet night.
It greets us with a warm embrace,
A gift of peace, a gentle grace.
And as we step inside tonight,
The wreath reminds us of the light.
Of Christmas cheer and love so true,
That's always here for me and you.

Poem 11: "The Christmas Parade"

The floats go by with music loud,
The streets are filled with every crowd.
The children cheer, their faces bright,
As the Christmas parade takes flight.
The dancers twirl, the drummers beat,
The bands march proudly down the street.
The bells ring out, the flags wave high,
As festive colors fill the sky.
The clowns perform, the reindeer prance,
The crowds begin to laugh and dance.
The joy of Christmas fills the air,
A magic moment, free and fair.
The snowflakes fall, the music plays,
As happy faces light the days.
The parade will travel far and wide,
With Christmas joy, we all collide.
Each float a picture, full of glee,
A celebration, full and free.
We wave and shout, our hearts aglow,
As Christmas spirit starts to show.
And when the parade comes to an end,
We know that Christmas is our friend.
Its love and cheer will never fade,
For Christmas joy will always invade.

Poem 12: "Reindeer Games"

The reindeer prance in snowy fields,
Their antlers strong, their spirit healed.
They race through clouds and skies so high,
With twinkling stars as their guide nearby.
Their hooves are swift, their noses bright,
They travel far into the night.
Through frosty air and swirling snow,
The reindeer play, their spirits glow.
They leap and bound, they twist and twirl,
Like Christmas lights that swirl and whirl.
Their laughter echoes through the sky,
As Santa's team prepares to fly.
The winter winds are soft and cold,
But the reindeer never seem too old.
They dash through snow, they glide with ease,
Their reindeer games, a festive breeze.
And as they rest on Christmas Eve,
They know that joy is theirs to weave.
For Christmas magic fills the air,
And reindeer games are everywhere.
So as you dream this Christmas night,
Remember those with hearts so bright.
The reindeer play with all their might,
To bring you joy on Christmas night.

Poem 13: "The Christmas Eve Night"

The moon is high, the stars are bright,
On Christmas Eve, the world feels right.
We gather 'round, our hearts in sync,
And share a quiet, peaceful drink.
The house is warm, the fire glows,
The world outside in stillness grows.
We wait for Santa, hopes held tight,
And count the stars through frosty night.
The stockings hang, the cookies set,
We whisper wishes we won't forget.
The magic hums, so soft and pure,
On Christmas Eve, we are secure.
The night is calm, the world asleep,
The stars above a vigil keep.
We wait in silence, hearts aflame,
For Christmas morning to reclaim.
The clock ticks on, the time is near,
We hold our breath, we hold our cheer.
For soon the world will wake and sing,
The joy that Christmas morning brings.
So close your eyes and dream away,
For Christmas will be here today.
The night is long, but joy is near,
On Christmas Eve, we have no fear.

Poem 14: "Gingerbread House"

We mix the dough, so warm and sweet,
For gingerbread, a tasty treat.
With frosting thick and candy bright,
We build our house by candlelight.
The walls go up, the roof is laid,
Each piece of candy finely made.
The icing swirls in every place,
A work of art, a sweet embrace.
The gumdrops line the windows bright,
The candy canes are pure delight.
The chocolate chips, the sugar spray,
Make our gingerbread house today.
We decorate with colors bold,
Our house a vision to behold.
A masterpiece of sugar dreams,
The sweetest house the world has seen.
The aroma fills the room with cheer,
Of Christmas warmth and love so near.
The house we've made, the joy we share,
A Christmas treasure beyond compare.
And when we eat it, piece by piece,
We'll savor joy and find release.
For gingerbread, with love and grace,
Is a gift of Christmas we embrace.

Poem 15: "The Nativity Scene"

In the stable, soft and bright,
A little baby, pure delight.
The manger holds the Savior's grace,
A symbol of God's loving face.
The animals kneel, the angels sing,
A holy night, a sacred ring.
The star above, so full of light,
Guides the way through peaceful night.
Mary smiles, so full of care,
Joseph's love is everywhere.
The world has come to see the child,
A king who makes the world go wild.
The shepherds kneel, the kings arrive,
To honor Him, who made us thrive.
The nativity, a sacred sight,
Fills our hearts with pure delight.
The gift of love, the gift of peace,
Is wrapped in joy, may it never cease.
The story told, the message clear,
That Christmas joy is ever near.
And as we stand by manger low,
We feel the love that will always grow.
The nativity brings peace so true,
A Christmas gift for me and you.

Poem 16: "The Snowflakes Fall"

The snowflakes dance, so soft, so light,
Drifting gently through the night.
They twirl and swirl in winter's glow,
Covering the earth below.
Each flake unique, a work of art,
A masterpiece that's set apart.
They settle gently, soft as lace,
A winter's kiss, a sweet embrace.
The trees are dressed in coats of white,
The world aglow in quiet light.
The snowflakes sing a song so pure,
Of peace and love, they all endure.
The wind whispers, soft and clear,
As snowflakes fall, year after year.
They blanket earth in snowy grace,
A Christmas wonder, full of space.
We catch them gently on our tongues,
And listen to their silent songs.
The snowflakes fall, the world stands still,
A peaceful moment, hearts do fill.
And as they fall, the world is bright,
A Christmas dream, a pure delight.
The snowflakes teach us, if we try,
To see the beauty in the sky.

Poem 17: "The Christmas Tree"

The Christmas tree stands tall and bright,
Adorned with ornaments of light.
Its branches full, its trunk so strong,
A symbol of where hearts belong.
The star on top, so full of grace,
A guiding light in every space.
The lights blink softly, one by one,
A shimmering glow that's second to none.
The tinsel sparkles, silver, gold,
A tree of wonder, pure and bold.
Each ornament a tale to tell,
Of Christmas joy that rings so well.
The presents lie beneath its base,
A treasure trove, a warm embrace.
The tree reflects the joy we share,
A memory of love laid bare.
We gather close, our hearts entwined,
Around the tree, our souls aligned.
The Christmas tree, a shining dream,
Fills every heart with Christmas gleam.
And when the lights flicker bright,
We know that Christmas is in sight.
The tree, so full of joy and cheer,
Will stay with us throughout the year.

Poem 18: "The Gift of Giving"

The best of gifts cannot be bought,
It's something deeper, something sought.
The gift of love, the gift of care,
The gift of kindness, always there.
A smile, a hug, a helping hand,
A gift of joy, that will withstand.
The gift of time, the gift of heart,
A treasure that will never part.
Wrapped with love, no ribbon needed,
A simple gift, our hearts have pleaded.
For giving brings the greatest cheer,
A joy that grows year after year.
The laughter shared, the memories made,
The bonds we've formed that will not fade.
For giving is the Christmas way,
And joy will bloom on Christmas day.
So as you give, remember true,
The gift of giving lives in you.
The more you give, the more you see,
That Christmas lives eternally.

Poem 19: "The Christmas Angel"

An angel hovers in the sky,
With golden wings that gently fly.
Her voice is soft, her heart so pure,
She whispers peace that will endure.
She watches over all below,
Her halo gleams with steady glow.
Her wings are soft, her smile so kind,
A Christmas gift, a peace of mind.
She flies above the snowy land,
A gentle touch, a guiding hand.
Her presence fills the starry night,
And fills our hearts with pure delight.
She sings a song of joy and cheer,
A Christmas tune for all to hear.
The angel's love, so bright and true,
Is given to both me and you.
She guides us through the night so long,
Her voice, a soft and heavenly song.
The Christmas angel, pure and bright,
Is with us on this holy night.
So when you see the stars up high,
Remember that the angels fly.
They carry peace, they carry light,
On Christmas Eve, through every night.

Poem 20: "The Snowy Morning"

The morning comes with snow so bright,
A blanket soft, a pure delight.
The world is still, the air so cold,
A wondrous sight, a joy untold.
The trees are wrapped in frosty white,
The sun peeks through, a soft, warm light.
The birds take flight, the wind does blow,
As Christmas joy begins to grow.
We step outside and feel the chill,
But hearts are warm and spirits still.
We make our marks in snow so deep,
As Christmas magic stirs from sleep.
The morning sparkles, full of cheer,
A snowy wonder drawing near.
We breathe in deep, the air so pure,
A Christmas moment, rich and sure.
The world is bright with winter's charm,
A Christmas morn that feels so warm.
And as we walk, we hold in sight,
The magic of this snowy light.

Poem 21: "Santa's Workshop"

In Santa's shop, the elves do cheer,
Preparing toys for all to hear.
They hammer, paint, and sew with care,
To fill the world with joy to spare.
From dolls to trains, from books to games,
Each gift is made with love that flames.
The elves work hard, with joy and glee,
A magical place for all to see.
The clock ticks down, the work is near,
The toys are ready, Christmas cheer.
Santa's sleigh will soon take flight,
And fill the world with Christmas light.
The elves all pause, their work is done,
The workshop glows beneath the sun.
And as they rest, they know so well,
Their gift of joy will surely swell.
For Santa's workshop, full of dreams,
Is where the Christmas spirit gleams.
And every toy, from hand to heart,
Is a symbol of a joyful start.

Poem 22: "The Christmas Star"

A star shines bright, so far, so near,
A guiding light to bring us cheer.
It shines above the world so wide,
A beacon of hope, shining bright.
The star of Christmas, pure and true,
Brings joy to me, and joy to you.
It lights the way for hearts so bright,
A symbol of the Christmas night.
It sparkles high, it twinkles bright,
A guide to love and joy and light.
It shows us hope, it shows us grace,
A shining gift, a holy place.
The Christmas star, so pure, so kind,
Reminds us all to be aligned.
With love and joy, with hearts so pure,
The Christmas star will long endure.
So when you see the star up high,
Know that Christmas will never die.
It shines for all who seek its glow,
A Christmas star, aglow below.

Poem 23: "The Christmas Eve Wish"

On Christmas Eve, we close our eyes,
And send our wishes to the skies.
We dream of snow, of lights that glow,
And love that sets our hearts aglow.
The twinkling stars, the moon so bright,
Fill our hearts with pure delight.
A Christmas wish, a hopeful dream,
That everything is as it seems.
The world is still, the night is deep,
The secrets of the night we keep.
We whisper wishes soft and clear,
For Christmas joy to draw near.
Our hearts are filled with hope and grace,
As we await the morning's face.
For Christmas brings a special cheer,
A wish fulfilled, a love sincere.
The clock ticks on, the minutes fly,
Our dreams take wings, they soar and sigh.
And when the morning light does show,
Our Christmas wishes start to grow.
So as you wish, remember true,
That Christmas dreams are meant for you.
They fill our hearts with light and cheer,
A wish come true, year after year.

Poem 24: "The Christmas Carol"

The carolers sing through frosty air,
Their voices pure, their hearts laid bare.
They sing of peace, of joy, of light,
On this most holy Christmas night.
Their song is sweet, their voices clear,
A melody that all can hear.
The words of love, the tune of grace,
Fill every heart, every space.
They walk through streets with hearts aglow,
Their carols soft, their faces glow.
The joy of Christmas fills the night,
As carolers bring the world delight.
Each note they sing, each word they say,
Spreads joy and love along the way.
Their carol is a gift of cheer,
That warms the heart and draws it near.
So when you hear a carol sung,
Let joy arise, let hearts be young.
For Christmas carols, full of grace,
Bring Christmas magic to every place.
And though the song may fade away,
Its love and cheer will always stay.
For in the carol, hearts do see,
The joy and peace of Christmas free.

Poem 25: "The Christmas Lights"

The Christmas lights begin to glow,
Twinkling softly in the snow.
They light the streets, they light the trees,
Filling the world with warmth and ease.
The colors sparkle, bright and bold,
A magic tale that must be told.
From red to green, to blue and white,
The Christmas lights shine through the night.
They blink and twirl, they glow and shine,
Each light a star, so pure, divine.
They warm the hearts, they light the way,
For Christmas joy that comes to stay.
We drive through towns and cities bright,
The Christmas lights in pure delight.
Each home adorned, each yard aglow,
A sight that fills us deep below.
The lights bring cheer, the lights bring love,
A gift from heaven up above.
They shine through every night and day,
A Christmas gift that's here to stay.
So when you see the lights so bright,
Remember Christmas, full of light.
For in the glow, we see the truth,
That Christmas brings us joy and youth.

Poem 26: "The Christmas Snowman"

We build a snowman, tall and grand,
With a carrot nose and mittened hand.
A scarf of red, a hat so blue,
Our snowman is a friend so true.
We roll the snow, so soft and deep,
Into a ball, a mound to keep.
The snowman smiles, his eyes so bright,
A Christmas joy, a pure delight.
The frosty air, the winter's chill,
Don't stop the fun, don't stop the thrill.
We build with laughter, build with glee,
A snowy friend for you and me.
The snowman stands, a watchful friend,
He'll greet the dawn and see the end.
But as we go, we leave behind,
A winter treasure, peace of mind.
And when the sun begins to rise,
Our snowman waves with snowy eyes.
He'll melt away with morning light,
But in our hearts, he's still in sight.
So when you build your snowman tall,
Remember joy is best of all.
For in the snow, we find delight,
A Christmas friend to greet the night.

Poem 27: "The Christmas Cookie"

The cookies bake, the house smells sweet,
A treat for all, a Christmas feat.
The dough is soft, the sugar bright,
We bake with love on Christmas night.
The shapes we cut, the sprinkles spread,
A work of art from dough and bread.
We make them round, we make them tall,
We make them all, big and small.
The oven hums, the warmth inside,
Fills our hearts with Christmas pride.
The cookies bake, they rise so high,
Until they're golden, warm, and dry.
We ice them with a sweet, soft glaze,
And decorate in festive ways.
Each cookie's perfect, each one sweet,
A treat that's sure to be a treat.
We leave some out for Santa, too,
With milk beside, a gift so true.
For Santa loves a cookie bite,
A Christmas joy, a sweet delight.
So bake some cookies, share with cheer,
A Christmas gift that's always near.
For in the cookies, love we find,
A taste of joy, a peace of mind.

Poem 28: "The Christmas Stockings"

We hang the stockings by the fire,
With hope and joy, our hearts aspire.
Each one filled with treats and dreams,
A gift from Santa, so it seems.
The stockings sway, the fire glows,
A warmth that spreads, a love that grows.
We peek inside to see the cheer,
As Christmas morning draws near.
A candy cane, a toy so bright,
A little gift, a pure delight.
Each stocking filled with thought and care,
A token of love everywhere.
We hang them high, we hang them proud,
A festive sight, a merry crowd.
The stockings tell a story true,
Of love and joy, and dreams anew.
And when we wake, the stockings full,
A Christmas miracle to pull.
The stockings bring us all together,
A Christmas gift that lasts forever.
So hang your stockings with delight,
For Christmas brings its purest light.
And when they're filled, you'll surely see,
The magic of the Christmas tree.

Poem 29: "The Christmas Countdown"

Each day we mark, the days to go,
Until Christmas comes with snow.
The calendar waits, the numbers tick,
We count the days, so full, so quick.
Each window opens, one by one,
The countdown clock, so full of fun.
We mark the days, the hours, too,
Until the Christmas bells ring true.
We wait with joy, we wait with glee,
For Christmas morning's mystery.
The gifts, the food, the fun to come,
The joy of Christmas, all become.
We cross the days, we count them down,
Until the day the bells resound.
The magic builds, the joy grows wide,
As Christmas nears, our hearts collide.
And when the day has come at last,
The wait is over, the joy is fast.
The countdown ends, the magic's here,
A Christmas day we hold so dear.
So mark your calendar, day by day,
Until Christmas comes to light the way.
For in the countdown, hearts do find,
A Christmas joy, so sweet, so kind.

Poem 30: "The Gingerbread House"

We bake a house, with icing sweet,
A candy roof, a cookie treat.
The walls are firm, the frosting thick,
The gingerbread house, built to stick.
The windows sparkle, candy bright,
Decorated with all our might.
We make it tall, we make it neat,
A gingerbread home, oh what a treat!
We add some gumdrops, red and green,
And licorice sticks, a Christmas scene.
The house so sweet, a joy to see,
A holiday wonder, full of glee.
We decorate it, top to base,
With sugary love and candy grace.
Each little detail, soft and bright,
Makes our gingerbread house a sight.
But when we're done, we take a bite,
The candy crisp, the cookies light.
Our gingerbread house, a memory dear,
A taste of joy we hold near.
So bake your house, so full of cheer,
And fill it with love, year after year.
For in the gingerbread you see,
A Christmas tale, for you and me.

Poem 31: "The Christmas Parade"

The Christmas parade marches down,
Through the snowy, wintry town.
With floats so bright, and bands that play,
The joy of Christmas lights the way.
The dancers twirl in sparkling clothes,
The bells ring out, the music flows.
The children cheer, their faces bright,
As the parade brings pure delight.
Santa waves from his grand sleigh,
The reindeer prance and dance today.
The crowd all claps, the spirits high,
As Christmas cheer fills up the sky.
The marching bands, the drummers beat,
The Christmas parade can't be beat!
The clowns and jesters dance around,
Their laughter lifts the joyful sound.
So join the parade, come one, come all,
A Christmas celebration, big and small.
The Christmas parade brings us together,
To celebrate this joyful weather.
And when the parade has passed on by,
We smile and wave, and say goodbye.
For the spirit of Christmas, so sweet and true,
Lives in the hearts of me and you.

Poem 32: "The Christmas Wish List"

I write my list, all full of cheer,
Of toys and treats I'd like this year.
A doll, a train, a shiny bike,
A gift to make my Christmas bright.
I scribble fast, I write with care,
My Christmas wishes in the air.
A wish for peace, a wish for love,
A wish for joy to rise above.
The list is long, the paper wide,
But in my heart, love does reside.
For Christmas gifts, though they are nice,
The gift of love is worth more than price.
I hand my list with hopes so high,
And watch it twirl up to the sky.
I trust that Santa will come through,
With all the magic, just for you.
But most of all, my wish, I say,
Is for a world of peace today.
A Christmas wish for all to share,
A world of kindness, everywhere.
So write your list, don't forget,
The Christmas spirit's in your heart, set.
For gifts can fade, and toys may break,
But love and joy, those gifts we make.

Poem 33: "The Christmas Tree Farm"

We drive to the tree farm, near and far,
In search of the perfect Christmas star.
Among the pines, the firs so tall,
We look for the tree that beats them all.
The trees stand still, in rows so neat,
Each one a prize, a Christmas treat.
We search and search, we stand and gaze,
Until we find the perfect prize.
We cut it down, with care and grace,
The Christmas tree, our hearts do race.
We haul it home, so full of cheer,
The Christmas tree will soon be here.
We decorate with love and light,
The tree aglow on Christmas night.
The ornaments hang, the lights do shine,
Our tree's a joy, so bright, divine.
And as we sit and gaze with pride,
The Christmas tree, our hearts collide.
It stands as proof of love and joy,
A Christmas miracle to enjoy.
So visit the farm, find your tree,
A symbol of love and unity.
For Christmas trees bring peace and cheer,
A memory to last all year.

Poem 34: "The Christmas Eve Bell"

The bell rings out on Christmas Eve,
A sound so sweet, we all believe.
Its chime is soft, yet full of cheer,
A bell of love, so close, so near.
It rings to mark the start of night,
A bell that calls the world to light.
Its song is pure, its tone so clear,
A Christmas bell, a sound so dear.
The bell will ring on Christmas morn,
To welcome in the day we've sworn.
A gift of hope, a gift of grace,
A Christmas bell that lights the place.
We wait in silence, hearts aligned,
For Christmas Eve is here, defined.
The bell does toll, its song so bright,
A harbinger of Christmas light.
So when you hear the Christmas bell,
Know that Christmas dreams do swell.
For in its ring, the love we feel,
Is Christmas magic, bright and real.
And when the bell has softly ceased,
We know that Christmas joy's released.
The bell rings out, our hearts do swell,
For Christmas love, we know so well.

Poem 35: "The Christmas Morning"

The Christmas morning, bright and new,
With sparkling snow and skies so blue.
We wake with joy, our hearts so light,
The magic of this special night.
The presents wait beneath the tree,
Wrapped with love, for you and me.
We open them with cheers and glee,
The joy of Christmas, wild and free.
The breakfast table's full of cheer,
With pancakes, syrup, warmth so near.
We gather round, our hearts entwined,
A Christmas morning, pure, divine.
The laughter spills, the smiles are wide,
As Christmas joy fills up the tide.
We hug, we kiss, we share our day,
The Christmas magic here to stay.
So cherish each and every part,
Of Christmas morning, full of heart.
For in its glow, we come to see,
The magic of Christmas, wild and free.

Poem 36: "The North Pole"

To the North Pole, we travel far,
Past the clouds, past the stars.
Through icy winds and frosty skies,
We see the magic in Santa's eyes.
The elves are busy, working fast,
Building toys to make joy last.
Santa's sleigh is waiting near,
Ready for the night to cheer.
The snowflakes twirl, the winds do howl,
The reindeer rest beneath the prowl.
The Northern lights, they glow so bright,
Guiding Santa through the night.
The North Pole sparkles, cold and clear,
A land of wonder, full of cheer.
And there we see, amidst the snow,
The spirit of Christmas brightly glow.
So dream of the North Pole so true,
Where magic thrives and dreams come through.
For in that land, so far away,
The Christmas spirit will always stay.

Poem 37: "The Snowflake Dance"

The snowflakes twirl from skies so high,
They dance and twirl, they swirl and fly.
Each one unique, a work of art,
Falling down to warm each heart.
They drift and glide, they kiss the ground,
A gentle touch, without a sound.
They blanket earth in soft embrace,
A Christmas gift, a frosty grace.
We watch them dance, so free, so light,
As winter paints the world in white.
The snowflakes swirl with joyful glee,
A winter's dance for you and me.
The trees are dressed in snowy lace,
The world transformed, a magic place.
Each snowflake lands, a fleeting kiss,
A moment of pure, winter bliss.
So catch a snowflake, make a wish,
For Christmas dreams are always swish.
And as they fall, remember true,
The joy of Christmas comes to you.

Poem 38: "The Christmas Wreath"

The Christmas wreath, so full of cheer,
With holly leaves, so bright and clear.
A circle of love, a symbol true,
Of Christmas joy, forever new.
The red and green, the gold and white,
A wreath that shines in festive light.
We hang it high, we hang it proud,
A wreath that makes the season loud.
The holly berries, red and bright,
Shine like stars on Christmas night.
The wreath brings peace, it brings delight,
A gift of joy, a welcome sight.
We place it on the door so wide,
A symbol of the love inside.
The wreath reminds us, year by year,
That Christmas joy is always near.
So hang your wreath with love and care,
And spread its magic everywhere.
For in the wreath, we come to see,
The Christmas spirit, wild and free.

Poem 39: "The Christmas Fire"

The fire crackles, warm and bright,
A cozy glow on Christmas night.
The flames dance high, the embers glow,
As Christmas cheer begins to show.
We gather round, the fire's heat,
A perfect way to rest our feet.
The crackling wood, the softest sound,
The Christmas warmth that does abound.
We sip our cocoa, warm and sweet,
And talk of memories we repeat.
The fire's glow, the warmth it brings,
Is like the joy that Christmas sings.
Outside the snow begins to fall,
But in the fire, we stand tall.
The warmth we share, the love we know,
Keeps Christmas cheer within our glow.
So sit beside the fire's light,
And feel the magic of the night.
For in the warmth, we come to see,
That Christmas love is here to be.

Poem 40: "The Christmas Angels"

The angels sing on Christmas Eve,
Their voices pure, they do not grieve.
They sing of love, they sing of light,
A melody that fills the night.
Their wings are soft, their eyes so bright,
They watch us through the peaceful night.
They guide our hearts, they guide our ways,
And bring us peace through all our days.
With each sweet note, they fill the air,
A song of joy, a song of care.
They sing of hope, they sing of grace,
A Christmas gift for every place.
So when you hear that angel song,
Know that the angels all belong.
They fill our hearts with love and light,
And guide us through the silent night.
For angels bring us peace and cheer,
A Christmas gift that's always near.
So listen close, and you will find,
The angels' song will fill your mind.

Poem 41: "The Christmas Cookie Jar"

The cookie jar is filled with cheer,
With sugar, spice, and Christmas near.
The cookies smell so warm and sweet,
A perfect holiday treat to eat.
We roll the dough and cut the shapes,
From candy canes to Santa's capes.
We bake them golden, soft and light,
A Christmas joy that feels just right.
We add the sprinkles, dust the glaze,
Decorate in festive ways.
Each cookie's perfect, crisp and sweet,
A holiday snack, a Christmas treat.
The jar is full, the cookies bright,
We share them with all our might.
A bite of Christmas in each taste,
A treat that never goes to waste.
So fill your jar with love and care,
And share your cookies everywhere.
For Christmas cookies, made with glee,
Are a gift of joy for you and me.

Poem 42: "The Christmas Market"

We walk through stalls of Christmas cheer,
The market bright, the lights so near.
The smell of pine, the scents of sweet,
Fill the air and warm our feet.
The lights are strung on every tree,
A sight for all the world to see.
The vendors smile, the children play,
As Christmas joy fills up the day.
We buy some treats, we share a laugh,
The market's bustle never slack.
The warmth of love, the gift of light,
Makes everything feel just so right.
We see the crafts, the toys, the sweets,
A Christmas market, full of treats.
With every step, a joy unfolds,
A Christmas tale that's truly told.
So visit the market, near and far,
And let your heart be like a star.
For in the market, joy does grow,
And Christmas cheer begins to show.

Poem 43: "The Christmas Stocking Surprise"

We hang our stockings on the wall,
So Santa knows, we've done it all.
Each sock so big, so full of cheer,
A Christmas surprise, drawing near.
The stockings wait with open arms,
To hold the gifts and little charms.
Each one a promise, soft and bright,
That Christmas morning will take flight.
We hang them high, we hang them low,
A place for treasures, wrapped in glow.
And when we wake on Christmas day,
The stockings are a joy to sway.
A candy cane, a toy, a note,
A gift of love, we all devote.
The stockings filled with tender care,
A Christmas gift that's always there.
So hang your stocking, wide and high,
For Christmas magic fills the sky.
And when you wake to see the prize,
You'll find your joy in Christmas skies.

Poem 44: "The Christmas Carolers"

The carolers sing, their voices sweet,
A melody for all to greet.
They walk through streets, so cold, so bright,
And fill the world with Christmas light.
They sing of peace, they sing of joy,
A song for every girl and boy.
Their voices echo through the night,
A harmony, a love so bright.
The carolers walk from door to door,
Their song a gift that we adore.
The people smile, their hearts so warm,
As Christmas joy does take its form.
So when you hear a carol sing,
Join in the song and let it ring.
For Christmas carols, full of cheer,
Bring love and joy to all who hear.

Poem 45: "The Snowman's Hat"

We build a snowman, big and tall,
A carrot nose, a scarf, a ball.
His hat sits snug upon his head,
A frosty friend with joy to spread.
The snowflakes fall, they dust his hat,
A winter's crown, so sleek and flat.
His eyes are coal, so shiny bright,
A snowman's joy, a pure delight.
We smile and wave, we cheer and sing,
For the snowman's joy, he'll always bring.
Though he's made of snow and ice,
His heart is warm, his spirit nice.
The hat stays snug, the scarf so neat,
A winter look, a Christmas treat.
Our snowman stands, so proud, so bright,
A friend who shares in Christmas light.
So build your snowman, make him tall,
And give him joy, the best of all.
For in his hat, you'll always see,
A Christmas friend for you and me.

Poem 46: "The Christmas Lights"

The Christmas lights, they shine so bright,
A rainbow of colors, full of light.
They twinkle and blink, a cheerful sight,
Bringing joy to every night.
The trees are covered in bright arrays,
Lighting up our wintry days.
Each light a spark of Christmas cheer,
A glow of love to bring us near.
The lights shine down from high above,
A shining symbol of Christmas love.
They flicker, they glow, they softly gleam,
A holiday magic, a timeless dream.
We decorate our homes with pride,
Letting Christmas joy reside.
Each bulb a wish, a hope, a prayer,
That Christmas love is everywhere.
So when you see the Christmas glow,
Know that love and magic flow.
For in the lights, we all can find,
A Christmas peace, so sweet, so kind.

Poem 47: "The Christmas Countdown"

The days tick down, so full of cheer,
As Christmas Day draws near, so near.
We mark the days with joy and glee,
Counting down the time, you see.
Each day a treat, a gift, a rhyme,
A reason to make Christmas shine.
With every tick, we smile and wait,
For Christmas joy to celebrate.
The calendar shows the days so bright,
Each number crossed, a joyful sight.
The countdown's fun, the days go fast,
As Christmas magic comes at last.
The waiting builds, our hearts so true,
As Christmas comes, it brings us through.
The countdown ends, the day is here,
Christmas morning, full of cheer.
So count the days, don't miss a beat,
For Christmas time is oh so sweet.
And when the countdown finally ends,
The Christmas joy, it never bends.

Poem 48: "The Christmas Snowball"

We roll the snow into a ball,
It gets so big, we can't recall.
We toss it high, we toss it far,
A snowy gift from the North Star.
The snowball rolls, it gathers fast,
A winter treasure, made to last.
We chase it down, we laugh and play,
Until the snowball rolls away.
We pack it tight, we give a shove,
A Christmas snowball made with love.
We toss it high into the air,
A snowy gift without a care.
The snowflakes fall, the ball so bright,
A wintry treasure, pure delight.
We play together, full of cheer,
For Christmas magic, ever near.
So roll your snowball, make it high,
And watch it dance beneath the sky.
For in the snowball, you will see,
A gift of joy for you and me.

Poem 49: "The Christmas Carol"

Sing a Christmas carol loud,
Let the music fill the crowd.
A melody of love so true,
A gift of joy for me and you.
The carols echo through the night,
With voices strong, with hearts alight.
Each note a prayer, a song, a cheer,
For Christmas magic drawing near.
We sing of peace, we sing of light,
A carol's tune so soft, so bright.
The words are warm, the melody sweet,
A song that makes our hearts complete.
The carolers stand, the choir sings,
Their voices spread on angel's wings.
We join the song, our voices blend,
A Christmas carol, love we send.
So sing along, with joy and cheer,
For Christmas carols bring us near.
The song of love, the tune of peace,
A Christmas carol that won't cease.

Poem 50: "The Christmas Eve Sky"

The sky on Christmas Eve so wide,
Is full of stars that brightly guide.
The moon shines down, the night so clear,
A magical moment, full of cheer.
The stars twinkle, the sky is bright,
A Christmas glow that fills the night.
We look above, we pause and sigh,
At the beauty of the Christmas sky.
The air is cold, the wind is still,
As Christmas joy begins to fill.
We know that Santa's on his way,
Guided by the stars today.
The night is calm, the sky aglow,
As Christmas love begins to flow.
The stars above, they shine so bright,
Guiding Santa through the night.
So look above, on Christmas Eve,
And in the sky, you will believe.
For in the stars, so clear and wide,
The spirit of Christmas will reside.

Poem 51: "The Christmas Letter"

We write our letters, full of cheer,
To Santa Claus, so far, so near.
We write of wishes, dreams, and hope,
A letter filled with joy to cope.
We tell him all we'd like to see,
A gift, a wish, a Christmas tree.
We share our hearts, we share our love,
A Christmas letter sent above.
The paper's bright, the ink so bold,
A Christmas story to be told.
We seal it tight, we send it high,
To Santa's home, up in the sky.
We know that Santa reads them all,
And answers each one, big or small.
Our Christmas letter, full of care,
Is sent with love to everywhere.
So write your letter, make a wish,
For Christmas magic, pure and swish.
And when it's sent, so full of glee,
You'll know your heart is full, you see.

Poem 52: "The Christmas Tree Lights"

The Christmas tree lights up the room,
With colors bright that chase the gloom.
They twinkle and shine, so soft, so bright,
A holiday wonder, pure delight.
The bulbs they flash in reds and greens,
A Christmas glow, a magic scene.
The lights they blink, they softly glow,
A Christmas charm we all know.
We sit and watch the lights shine bright,
As Christmas joy fills up the night.
Each flicker soft, each glow so true,
The Christmas lights, a gift for you.
We gather 'round the tree so grand,
A family joy, hand in hand.
The lights they twinkle, the tree does gleam,
A Christmas magic, like a dream.
So let the Christmas lights shine bright,
And fill your heart with pure delight.
For in their glow, we all can see,
The magic of Christmas, wild and free.

Poem 53: "The Gingerbread House"

We bake a house, so sweet and bright,
With candy walls and frosting white.
The gingerbread, it smells so good,
A holiday treat, just like we should.
We decorate with gumdrops, too,
And sprinkle sugar, just for you.
The frosting glistens in the light,
A gingerbread house, pure delight.
We build it tall, we build it neat,
With candy doors and sugary feet.
The windows sparkle, the roof so sweet,
A Christmas treat that can't be beat.
We take a bite, the flavor's pure,
A tasty holiday, that's for sure.
The house may crumble, the candy fall,
But it's the joy that matters most of all.
So bake a house with love and care,
And share the joy, it's everywhere.
For gingerbread brings love and cheer,
And Christmas joy will always be near.

Poem 54: "The Christmas Parade"

The Christmas parade is marching down,
Through every street, through every town.
The floats are bright, the music loud,
A joyful celebration, big and proud.
The drummers beat, the horns they play,
As Santa's sleigh comes down the way.
The dancers twirl, the children smile,
The parade's excitement, all the while.
The snowflakes fall, the bells they ring,
As Christmas carolers start to sing.
The crowd all cheers, the joy is real,
A Christmas parade, the best appeal.
The elves wave high, the reindeer fly,
And Santa's sleigh is up so high.
The joy spreads far, the cheer so wide,
The Christmas parade's a joyful ride.
So join the parade, and march with cheer,
For Christmas joy is always near.
The parade's a wonder, a festive scene,
A holiday dream, so pure and keen.

Poem 55: "The Christmas Countdown Calendar"

Each day we open, one by one,
The little doors, oh, so much fun!
The Christmas calendar, full of cheer,
A holiday treasure drawing near.
Each window hides a little treat,
A chocolate surprise, so sweet to eat.
We count the days with joy and glee,
As Christmas grows so patiently.
The little doors are filled with dreams,
And candy stars that softly gleam.
Each tiny gift, a happy clue,
That Christmas joy is coming through.
We open doors and share a smile,
The countdown makes the wait worthwhile.
With every gift, we grow more bright,
As Christmas day comes into sight.
So count each day, enjoy the fun,
For Christmas joy has just begun.
The calendar's magic, the joy, the cheer,
Makes Christmas time feel oh so near.

Poem 56: "The Christmas Choir"

The choir sings so pure and bright,
Their voices shining in the night.
A melody that fills the air,
A song of love beyond compare.
The harmonies, they weave and soar,
A Christmas tune forever more.
The choir's voices rise and swell,
And in their song, we all can tell.
They sing of peace, they sing of cheer,
A Christmas song that's ever near.
Their voices blend, their hearts unite,
A melody that feels so right.
The notes are sweet, the carols strong,
Their music fills the Christmas song.
The choir sings with all their might,
Their voices glowing in the night.
So listen close and join the sound,
For Christmas cheer is all around.
The choir's song, so pure and bright,
Is a gift of love on Christmas night.

Poem 57: "The Christmas Story"

The Christmas story, told each year,
Of love and joy, and Christmas cheer.
The tale of Mary, brave and true,
And the baby born for me and you.
The star above, so bright and high,
Guided wise men from the sky.
They followed through the darkened night,
To bring their gifts, their hearts alight.
The angels sang, their voices sweet,
A Christmas message, pure and neat.
The shepherds came, they knelt to pray,
And found the child on Christmas Day.
The story told of peace and grace,
Of hope and love in every place.
The Christmas story, ever dear,
Is told again, year after year.
So gather round and hear the tale,
Of Christmas joy that will prevail.
For in this story, we can find,
The true Christmas spirit, pure and kind.

Poem 58: "The Christmas Carrot"

The reindeer need their treats so sweet,
A carrot snack is their big treat.
We leave it out with love and care,
For Santa's team, they'll be there.
The carrot bright, the perfect gift,
For reindeer hearts, it gives a lift.
They munch and nibble, full of cheer,
Preparing for their flight so near.
We leave the carrot by the door,
A gift for reindeer, nothing more.
Their noses bright, their antlers tall,
They work so hard, they give their all.
The Christmas carrot, sweet and true,
Is a gift for Santa's crew.
And as we sleep, they come and go,
To spread their magic in the snow.
So leave a carrot, give them love,
For they bring joy from high above.
The reindeer need their special treat,
And Christmas magic can't be beat.

Poem 59: "The Christmas Bells"

The Christmas bells, they ring so loud,
Their sound so pure, they lift the crowd.
With every chime, the joy does grow,
A Christmas cheer that we all know.
The bells ring out, they echo wide,
A melody from deep inside.
Their sound brings peace, their sound brings light,
A song that fills the silent night.
We hear the bells, we feel the joy,
A Christmas gift for girl and boy.
Their ringing sound, so full of cheer,
Brings Christmas love to all who hear.
The bells they toll, the bells they sing,
A song of peace that joy does bring.
So listen close, let your heart swell,
To the magic of the Christmas bell.
For in their chimes, we come to know,
That Christmas love will always grow.
The bells ring out, a joyful sound,
A Christmas magic all around.

Poem 60: "The Christmas Sleigh"

The Christmas sleigh, it glides so fast,
Through snowy skies, it's built to last.
With reindeer strong, and Santa too,
They race the night, to bring gifts to you.
The sleigh is pulled through snowy skies,
It travels fast, it flies so high.
Santa steers, the reins so tight,
Delivering joy on Christmas night.
The bells they jingle, the reins they sway,
As Santa travels on his way.
The sleigh, it glides on frosty air,
A Christmas journey full of care.
With every stop, with every glide,
The Christmas joy spreads far and wide.
The sleigh moves fast, it moves with grace,
Bringing Christmas magic to every place.
So watch the sky, and hear the cheer,
For Santa's sleigh is drawing near.
The reindeer gallop, the sleigh so bright,
Spreading Christmas joy through the night.

Poem 61: "The Christmas Stockings"

We hang our stockings by the door,
In hopes of treats and gifts galore.
Each one is filled with love and cheer,
A Christmas tradition, year by year.
The stockings wait, so soft and bright,
For Santa's gifts on Christmas night.
A candy cane, a shiny toy,
A little gift to bring pure joy.
We hang them up with hope and care,
Wondering what will be in there.
Each stocking holds a special surprise,
A moment of joy before our eyes.
The fire burns and softly glows,
As Christmas magic gently grows.
The stockings wait with hearts so warm,
For Santa's gifts in his big swarm.
So hang your stockings, neat and bright,
And wait for joy on Christmas night.
For in the stockings, love will be,
A Christmas gift for you and me.

Poem 62: "The Christmas Snowflakes"

Snowflakes fall, so soft, so white,
Dancing down in the pale moonlight.
Each one unique, a work of art,
A special gift, a Christmas heart.
They twirl and spin, they softly land,
A frosty gift from winter's hand.
The ground is covered, pure and bright,
With snowflakes making Christmas right.
We catch them on our tongues and smile,
And watch them fall in sparkling style.
Each one a treasure, cool and sweet,
A Christmas miracle at our feet.
The snowflakes fall and paint the sky,
A canvas blue, a winter's sigh.
Each flake a wish, a tiny prayer,
That Christmas joy will fill the air.
So watch the snowflakes, soft and light,
As they bring magic to the night.
For in their fall, we all can see,
A Christmas wonder, wild and free.

Poem 63: "The Christmas Cookies"

The oven hums, the cookies bake,
A sweet aroma we can't forsake.
With sugar, spice, and cinnamon too,
The Christmas cookies are coming through.
We roll the dough, we cut the shapes,
With stars and trees and little flakes.
The sprinkles shine, the frosting sweet,
A holiday treat that can't be beat.
We bake them crisp, we bake them warm,
With gingerbread, they take their form.
The cookies bake, the house smells great,
A holiday smell that's worth the wait.
We share the cookies, one by one,
Until the plate is nearly done.
Each bite a joy, each bite a cheer,
A Christmas treat we hold so dear.
So bake your cookies, share the love,
For they bring Christmas from above.
With every bite, we feel the cheer,
And Christmas joy is always near.

Poem 64: "The Christmas Magic"

The Christmas magic fills the air,
It's in the hearts, it's everywhere.
A little sprinkle, a dash of cheer,
Brings Christmas joy to all who are near.
It's in the lights that twinkle bright,
And in the peaceful, silent night.
It's in the laughter, the love, the song,
A magic that makes our hearts grow strong.
The Christmas magic, soft and true,
Wraps us in joy, through and through.
It fills the room, it fills the sky,
A Christmas spirit that will never die.
It's in the gifts, the hugs, the smiles,
The magic spreads for endless miles.
The Christmas magic, warm and pure,
A gift of love that will endure.
So feel the magic, close your eyes,
And let it fill you, just like the skies.
For Christmas magic, you will see,
Is love and joy for you and me.

Poem 65: "The Christmas Wreath"

We hang the wreath upon the door,
A symbol of Christmas, nothing more.
With holly leaves and berries bright,
It welcomes all to Christmas night.
The wreath is round, a perfect ring,
A Christmas joy, a song to sing.
It shows the love, it shows the cheer,
A Christmas symbol so sincere.
The greenery, the ribbon red,
A festive sight that fills the head.
The wreath is bright, it fills the air,
With Christmas joy beyond compare.
It welcomes guests, it welcomes friends,
The wreath is where our hearts ascend.
A holiday treasure, hung with care,
A Christmas wreath that fills the air.
So hang the wreath, and let it shine,
For Christmas joy will intertwine.
The wreath is love, the wreath is cheer,
A Christmas symbol year by year.

Poem 66: "The Christmas Angels"

The angels sing on Christmas Eve,
Their voices soft, they do believe.
They sing of love, they sing of peace,
A Christmas message, sweet release.
With wings of light, they soar above,
A heavenly choir, full of love.
Their voices rise in soft refrain,
Bringing joy to every lane.
The angels' song is full of grace,
A gentle light, a shining face.
They bring a blessing, pure and sweet,
A Christmas carol, soft and neat.
The angels guide the way ahead,
Their voices fill the skies, widespread.
With every note, we feel the light,
As angels bless the holy night.
So listen close, their song so near,
The angels' voice, a gift so clear.
Their Christmas cheer, a gift of love,
Sent from the angels high above.

Poem 67: "The Christmas Star"

The Christmas star shines high and bright,
A guiding light through silent night.
It leads the way for all to see,
A shining beacon, wild and free.
The star so bright, so pure, so clear,
It fills our hearts with Christmas cheer.
It lights the way to Bethlehem,
A shining star, a holy gem.
We follow it, our hearts aglow,
As Christmas joy begins to grow.
The star above, it shows the way,
To love and peace this Christmas Day.
The star will shine, it will not fade,
A Christmas light that's softly laid.
So when you see the star so bright,
Know that Christmas fills the night.
The Christmas star, a gift of grace,
Guides us to the holy place.
It lights the path, it fills the sky,
A Christmas treasure up so high.

Poem 68: "The Christmas Poinsettia"

The poinsettia, red and bright,
A Christmas flower, full of light.
Its petals shine with deep, bold hue,
A holiday gift that's pure and true.
The flower stands, so full of grace,
Its beauty shines in every space.
A symbol of love, so sweet and bright,
The poinsettia, a Christmas sight.
We place it on the mantel high,
A festive bloom beneath the sky.
Its colors bold, its fragrance sweet,
A perfect holiday treat.
The poinsettia brings joy and cheer,
A Christmas beauty so sincere.
Its colors warm, its spirit true,
A holiday joy for me and you.
So give a poinsettia with love and care,
For it will spread Christmas everywhere.
The flower bright, the Christmas bloom,
Fills every corner, fills every room.

Poem 69: "The Christmas Wish"

I wish for joy, I wish for peace,
I wish for Christmas to never cease.
I wish for love to fill the air,
And joy to spread from here to there.
I wish for laughter, soft and sweet,
I wish for friends and family to meet.
I wish for snowflakes, bright and true,
To cover the world in Christmas hue.
I wish for gifts, both big and small,
I wish for kindness to touch us all.
I wish for hearts to join and sing,
And make the Christmas bells ring.
I wish for Christmas to never end,
A time for joy with every friend.
I wish for love, I wish for cheer,
To carry us through every year.
So make a wish, just like me,
For Christmas joy to set us free.
A wish for Christmas, pure and bright,
To fill the world with love and light.

Poem 70: "The Snowman's Hat"

A snowman stands, so tall and grand,
With a carrot nose and mittened hand.
He wears a hat, so warm and bright,
A Christmas look, a pure delight.
The snowman smiles, his eyes aglow,
His frosty cheeks all covered in snow.
The hat sits snug upon his head,
A gift of warmth, his joy is spread.
We build him up with snow and care,
Adding buttons, giving him flair.
The hat completes his snowy look,
A Christmas style, that's off the hook!
The snowman watches, still and true,
As Christmas magic starts to brew.
His hat a symbol of Christmas cheer,
A season's joy that's drawing near.
So build a snowman, add a hat,
And share a smile, imagine that!
For snowmen bring a frosty glow,
That spreads the joy in Christmas snow.

Poem 71: "The Christmas Ribbon"

The Christmas ribbon, shiny bright,
It wraps the presents, pure delight.
It ties a bow, it makes a cheer,
A symbol of love and holiday near.
The ribbon curls, it sparkles bright,
A gift of joy, a Christmas sight.
We wrap it up, we tie it tight,
To make the Christmas feeling right.
The ribbon swirls in graceful arcs,
It adds a touch to Christmas sparks.
Each twist and turn, so neat and grand,
A perfect touch to lend a hand.
We tie the ribbon, soft and fine,
It adds the magic, pure design.
The Christmas ribbon is a sign,
Of joy and love, so sweet, divine.
So tie a ribbon, make it true,
And add the magic, just for you.
The ribbon's joy, so pure, so sweet,
A Christmas symbol that's complete.

Poem 72: "The Christmas Tree Ornaments"

We hang the ornaments with care,
Each one a treasure, bright and rare.
From glass to wood, from gold to red,
Each one tells a story, it's said.
The shiny balls, the twinkling lights,
The stars that shine so pure and bright.
Each ornament a memory dear,
A symbol of Christmas, year by year.
We hang them high, we hang them low,
Each one a gift, a love to show.
The angels, bells, the gifts, the sleigh,
All bring the magic of the day.
The ornaments sparkle, twirl and shine,
They add the magic, so divine.
A tree of love, a tree of cheer,
A Christmas treasure year by year.
So decorate with joy and grace,
And fill your heart with Christmas place.
For every ornament tells the tale,
Of Christmas joy that will not fail.

Poem 73: "The Christmas Train"

The Christmas train is on its way,
Through snowy fields, so bright and gay.
It whistles loud, it chugs along,
A Christmas ride, a merry song.
The cars are full of gifts and cheer,
With happy passengers, far and near.
The train moves fast, the wheels go round,
Spreading joy to every town.
The smokestack puffs, the whistle blows,
The Christmas train, it surely knows.
It travels fast, it travels far,
A Christmas journey like a star.
The lights they twinkle, soft and bright,
The train glides through the silent night.
A magic ride that we all take,
For Christmas joy is on the lake.
So hop aboard and take the ride,
With Christmas joy, we cannot hide.
The Christmas train, a festive sight,
Brings love and peace on Christmas night.

Poem 74: "The Christmas Carolers"

The carolers sing so sweet and loud,
Their voices bright, they stand so proud.
They sing of joy, they sing of peace,
A Christmas song that will not cease.
With songbooks open, they sing on high,
Their voices reaching to the sky.
They spread the cheer, they share the sound,
A Christmas melody all around.
They sing of snow, of love and light,
A Christmas tale so pure and bright.
Their harmony brings joy and cheer,
A carol song that we hold dear.
The carolers travel, door to door,
Their music fills the hearts, the floor.
A song of hope, a song of love,
A melody sent from heaven above.
So sing with joy, and share the cheer,
For Christmas carols bring us near.
The carolers' voices, sweet and true,
Fill every heart, both me and you.

Poem 75: "The Christmas Angel"

The Christmas angel, shining bright,
With wings of gold, so full of light.
She brings the peace, she brings the cheer,
A heavenly gift, so dear, so near.
Her voice is soft, her heart is kind,
She fills our souls, our hearts entwined.
With love and joy, she leads the way,
A Christmas angel on display.
She watches over, pure and true,
Her presence fills the sky so blue.
The angel's song, so sweet, divine,
A Christmas blessing, so refined.
She guides us through the darkest night,
With gentle wings and shining light.
The Christmas angel, pure and bright,
Brings peace to all, in Christmas's sight.
So follow the angel, pure and clear,
For Christmas joy is drawing near.
The angel's wings, the angel's song,
Will fill our hearts all Christmas long.

Poem 76: "The Christmas Gifts"

The Christmas gifts are wrapped with love,
They're sent with care, from heaven above.
Each one is special, full of cheer,
A gift of joy, a gift so dear.
From toys to books, from treats to clothes,
The Christmas gifts, they help us grow.
Each one a symbol of love and care,
A message of hope that we all share.
We give them freely, hearts so true,
For giving is what Christmas can do.
The joy it brings, the warmth it shows,
A gift of love that always grows.
So give a gift, with open heart,
And share the love, it's just the start.
For Christmas gifts are more than toys,
They're symbols of love, for girls and boys.
So wrap the gifts with joy and grace,
And fill the world with love's embrace.
The Christmas gifts, they come from heart,
A love and joy that will not part.

Poem 77: "The Christmas Morning"

The Christmas morning, fresh and bright,
The sun peeks through with soft light.
The stockings are empty, the gifts are near,
A joyful time, the best of the year.
The tree is lit, the bells they ring,
And children laugh, their hearts do sing.
We open gifts, we share a smile,
The Christmas morning is worth the while.
The joy it fills the morning air,
With love and cheer beyond compare.
A peaceful moment, sweet and true,
A gift of Christmas for me and you.
The breakfast table, set with care,
The joy of Christmas everywhere.
We gather round, our hearts so full,
For Christmas love is always beautiful.
So cherish the moment, hold it tight,
For Christmas morning's pure delight.
The joy, the peace, the love so true,
Christmas morning, just for you.

Poem 78: "The Christmas Magic of Giving"

The magic of Christmas is in the giving,
A heart that's open, so full of living.
A gift of love, a warm embrace,
A joyful smile upon each face.
We give our hearts, we give our time,
A simple gesture, so pure, so fine.
The magic of giving, sweet and true,
Makes Christmas bright for me and you.
It's not the gift that matters most,
But the love that we can proudly boast.
A gift of kindness, a gift of cheer,
Is all we need to draw near.
The magic is felt when we give with grace,
A gift of love, in every space.
For Christmas joy is in the heart,
A holiday miracle from the start.
So give with love, give with care,
For the Christmas magic is everywhere.
The joy of giving, pure and bright,
Brings peace and love on Christmas night.

Poem 79: "The Christmas Cookie Jar"

The cookie jar, so full and sweet,
With treats and candies, what a treat!
We bake the cookies, soft and warm,
A Christmas ritual, a joyful norm.
The jar is filled with shapes and sizes,
From gingerbread to sweet surprises.
The cookies sparkle, the frosting glows,
A festive treat that everyone knows.
We nibble cookies, warm and crisp,
Their sweetness fills our hearts with bliss.
Each bite a memory, each bite a cheer,
A Christmas tradition we hold dear.
The cookie jar, it never stays full,
For we eat the cookies, they're too wonderful.
But every Christmas, we bake again,
And fill the jar with joy and then...
So share the cookies, give a bite,
For the Christmas cookie jar's a delight.
Each cookie baked, each smile shared,
Brings holiday joy beyond compare.

Poem 80: "The Christmas Village"

The Christmas village, small and bright,
Is filled with wonders, pure delight.
With tiny houses, snow-covered roofs,
It's like a dream, a Christmas proof.
The people gather, small and sweet,
To share their joy on snowy streets.
The village shines with lights aglow,
A Christmas world we all know.
The tiny trees, the twinkling stars,
The little cars that drive so far.
Each little piece, a Christmas sight,
A miniature world that's pure delight.
We watch in awe, our hearts so warm,
As the village takes its festive form.
A world of cheer, a world so bright,
A Christmas wonder, day or night.
So visit the village, take a look,
At the tiny wonders in every nook.
The Christmas village, pure and true,
A holiday dream for me and you.

Poem 81: "The Christmas Parade"

The Christmas parade is on its way,
With floats and bands to start the day.
The people cheer, the music plays,
A joyful celebration that stays.
The floats are filled with gifts and cheer,
With sparkling lights that fill the air.
The band plays on, the crowd does sway,
As Christmas joy comes our way.
The dancers twirl, the singers sing,
The Christmas parade is such a thing!
With children laughing all around,
Christmas cheer is truly found.
The marching bands, the clowns, the snow,
The Christmas parade steals the show.
A joyful celebration for all to see,
A Christmas parade, wild and free.
So join the parade, and wave your hand,
For Christmas joy is in this land.
The Christmas parade, a festive sight,
Brings joy and love, all day and night.

Poem 82: "The Christmas Sleigh"

The Christmas sleigh rides through the snow,
With bells that jingle, soft and slow.
The reindeer fly, the driver steers,
As Christmas joy draws ever near.
The sleigh is filled with gifts and cheer,
For every child, far and near.
It slides through snow, with steady grace,
A Christmas ride we all embrace.
The jingles ring, the snowflakes fall,
The sleigh glides on, the bells call.
A festive journey, a wondrous ride,
A Christmas sleigh, with love inside.
The sleigh is swift, it moves so fast,
As Christmas magic seems to last.
Through frosty air, through winter's glow,
The sleigh brings joy wherever we go.
So hop on the sleigh, come join the fun,
The Christmas journey has just begun.
With joy and cheer, it will not stray,
The Christmas sleigh leads the way!

Poem 83: "The Christmas Bells"

The Christmas bells ring loud and clear,
Their joyous chime is music dear.
They toll for peace, they toll for love,
A sweet reminder from above.
The bells ring out on Christmas morn,
To celebrate the day we're born.
A gift of joy, a gift of light,
A sound that fills the holy night.
The bells they toll, they never tire,
Their music lifts, their voices higher.
A Christmas song that fills the air,
With love and joy beyond compare.
The bells they toll from steeple high,
As Christmas magic fills the sky.
Each toll a prayer, each toll a cheer,
A Christmas sound that we hold dear.
So listen closely, hear them ring,
For Christmas bells are what they bring.
A sound of love, a sound so sweet,
A Christmas melody, complete.

Poem 84: "The Christmas Carol"

We sing a Christmas carol bright,
To fill the world with Christmas light.
The notes they soar, the lyrics cheer,
A joyful tune, for all to hear.
The carolers sing, with hearts aglow,
Their voices rise, the praises flow.
A song of joy, a song of peace,
A Christmas carol never cease.
We join in chorus, one by one,
Until the carol has been sung.
A melody of pure delight,
To fill the world with Christmas light.
The carol echoes through the night,
A shining song of love so bright.
A melody so sweet and true,
For Christmas joy is here for you.
So sing your carol, sing it loud,
And join the chorus of the crowd.
For Christmas carols spread the cheer,
A joyful sound for all to hear.

Poem 85: "The Christmas Lantern"

The Christmas lantern glows so bright,
It lights the way through winter's night.
With candle glow and glass so clear,
It brings the magic of Christmas near.
The lantern flickers, soft and warm,
A peaceful light, a quiet charm.
It guides the way through frosty air,
A Christmas glow that's always there.
The light it shines through every street,
It makes the world feel so complete.
The lantern's glow, it spreads so far,
A Christmas light, a shining star.
We carry the lantern, shining bright,
As Christmas joy fills the night.
Its glow reminds us of the way,
To peace and love on Christmas Day.
So light the lantern, let it glow,
For Christmas joy is sure to grow.
The Christmas lantern, pure and true,
Brings joy and peace to me and you.

Poem 86: "The Christmas Wreath"

The Christmas wreath upon the door,
With holly leaves and berries galore.
It welcomes all with Christmas cheer,
A symbol of the love we hold dear.
The wreath is hung with tender care,
To greet the season everywhere.
With ribbon bows and pinecones neat,
It's a holiday decoration so sweet.
The green and red, the festive sight,
A wreath that glows with Christmas light.
It's a sign that Christmas has begun,
A welcoming joy for everyone.
The wreath spins round with holiday grace,
A symbol of warmth in every place.
Its circle of love, it never ends,
A Christmas wreath that always sends.
So hang the wreath and let it shine,
For Christmas love is truly divine.
The wreath reminds us, pure and bright,
That Christmas joy is in our sight.

Poem 87: "The Christmas Snowflake"

A snowflake falls, so soft, so light,
It dances down in Christmas night.
Each one a wonder, pure and bright,
A tiny miracle in the light.
No two the same, so unique they are,
Each snowflake twirls like a shining star.
They blanket the earth in soft white glow,
A Christmas gift from nature's flow.
The snowflakes fall, they swirl and glide,
A winter wonder, far and wide.
Each one a blessing, soft and pure,
A beauty of Christmas that will endure.
They gently land on trees and ground,
A Christmas wonder all around.
Each snowflake whispers in the air,
A message of Christmas everywhere.
So watch the snowflakes as they fall,
And listen closely to their call.
For Christmas snowflakes, soft and bright,
Bring peace and joy to every night.

Poem 88: "The Christmas Stocking"

The Christmas stocking on the wall,
So soft and red, so big and tall.
It waits for gifts, it waits for cheer,
A Christmas tradition, year by year.
We hang it high, we hang it proud,
For Santa's gifts, it draws a crowd.
Each stocking filled with sweet delight,
A symbol of joy, on Christmas night.
The treats inside, the gifts so sweet,
A Christmas stocking can't be beat.
With little toys and candy bars,
The stocking shines like Christmas stars.
We hang our stockings with such care,
For Santa's gifts will soon be there.
The stockings filled with dreams come true,
A Christmas gift just for me and you.
So hang your stockings, don't delay,
For Christmas magic's on its way!
The Christmas stocking, warm and bright,
Holds the joy of Christmas night.

Poem 89: "The Christmas Pudding"

The Christmas pudding on the plate,
A festive treat, it's truly great.
With spices warm and fruits so sweet,
It's a holiday favorite, can't be beat.
The pudding steamed and topped with cheer,
A dessert that brings the season near.
We gather 'round, we cut a slice,
A Christmas treat, so rich and nice.
The flavors blend, the taste so grand,
A pudding made by loving hand.
With brandy sauce, it's pure delight,
A Christmas joy on every bite.
We share the pudding, rich and sweet,
A Christmas tradition we repeat.
With every slice, the joy is spread,
A Christmas dessert that's full of bread.
So serve the pudding, warm and bright,
For Christmas joy fills the night.
The Christmas pudding, rich and sweet,
A holiday treat that's quite a feat.

Poem 90: "The Christmas Lights"

The Christmas lights, so bright they shine,
A twinkling sparkle, pure divine.
They light the house, the trees, the street,
A festive glow, so warm, so sweet.
The lights they twinkle in every hue,
From red and green to shades of blue.
They wrap the trees and line the walls,
A Christmas glow that surely calls.
The Christmas lights, they shine so bright,
They twinkle softly through the night.
A glow that fills the world with cheer,
A Christmas wonder we hold dear.
The lights on houses, big and small,
Decorate the street and all.
They shine with joy, they shine with love,
A Christmas blessing from above.
So light the lights, and let them glow,
For Christmas magic soon will show.
The Christmas lights, they twinkle bright,
Bringing joy through Christmas night.

Poem 91: "The Christmas Lullaby"

The Christmas lullaby, soft and sweet,
A gentle tune, a restful beat.
It lulls us to sleep on Christmas Eve,
With dreams of joy we can believe.
The melody is soft and pure,
A Christmas tune that will endure.
It fills the heart with love so deep,
And whispers peace as we fall asleep.
The lullaby flows like a breeze,
It wraps us up with gentle ease.
A song of peace, a song of light,
It guides us through the holy night.
The Christmas lullaby sings so sweet,
A perfect melody, pure and neat.
It brings us rest, it brings us peace,
A Christmas blessing, never cease.
So let the lullaby softly play,
And drift to sleep, so peaceful, gay.
The Christmas lullaby, so true,
Brings love and peace for me and you.

Poem 92: "The Christmas Angel's Message"

The Christmas angel's message clear,
A song of peace, a love sincere.
She sings of joy, she sings of light,
A Christmas message, pure and bright.
Her wings they flutter in the air,
A sign of hope beyond compare.
She whispers softly in our ear,
A message of Christmas, drawing near.
The angel's voice is soft and true,
It brings a gift for me and you.
A message of love, a song of peace,
A Christmas blessing that won't cease.
She flies on high with joy and grace,
A smile of peace on her sweet face.
The Christmas angel, pure and bright,
Brings us love on Christmas night.
So listen close to the angel's song,
For it fills our hearts and makes us strong.
The Christmas message, clear and true,
Is peace and love for me and you.

Poem 93: "The Christmas Tree Lights"

The Christmas tree lights softly glow,
A twinkling wonder, gentle show.
Each light a star, each light a dream,
A Christmas wonder, bright and gleam.
The lights they sparkle on the tree,
A shining sight for all to see.
They twinkle, twirl, and softly gleam,
A Christmas wonder, like a dream.
The tree is full of colors bright,
Each bulb a ray of Christmas light.
The ornaments catch the glow,
A festive tree that steals the show.
The lights shine on, they flicker bright,
A symbol of Christmas joy and light.
They fill the air with festive cheer,
A Christmas glow that draws us near.
So decorate the tree with lights,
And watch them sparkle through the nights.
The Christmas tree, so bright and true,
Brings love and joy for me and you.

Poem 94: "The Christmas Joy in Our Hearts"

The Christmas joy is in our hearts,
It fills the world with happy starts.
With love and kindness, pure and true,
It makes the Christmas dream come through.
We share the joy, we share the cheer,
For Christmas joy is ever near.
It lifts our spirits, fills our days,
And fills our hearts with warm displays.
The joy of Christmas, shining bright,
It fills the world with pure delight.
It's in our hearts, it's in our song,
A love for Christmas that is strong.
We spread the joy to every friend,
A Christmas cheer that will not end.
The joy of Christmas fills the air,
A love so pure, so kind, so rare.
So hold the joy within your heart,
For Christmas love will never part.
The Christmas joy, it's pure and true,
A gift of love for me and you.

Poem 95: "The Christmas Eve Stars"

The Christmas Eve stars shine so bright,
They twinkle softly in the night.
A sky of wonder, pure and high,
A Christmas miracle in the sky.
The stars above, they light the way,
For Santa's sleigh on Christmas Day.
They guide him through the frosty air,
A shining beacon everywhere.
The stars they gleam, they shine, they glow,
A sparkling beauty in the snow.
They twinkle bright on Christmas Eve,
A gift of love, we all believe.
Each star a wish, each star a dream,
A shining light, a Christmas beam.
The stars above, they bless the night,
And fill our hearts with pure delight.
So look above on Christmas Eve,
And see the stars, and do believe.
For Christmas Eve stars are bright,
And bring us joy on Christmas night.

Poem 96: "The Christmas Story"

The Christmas story, pure and true,
It tells of love and joy anew.
A child was born on this bright day,
To light the world in every way.
The story begins with humble grace,
A star that shines in a darkened place.
The angels sing, the shepherds pray,
A Christmas story, on display.
A manger, a babe, a mother's smile,
The Christmas story, told in style.
A story of peace, a story of hope,
A story to help us all cope.
The story of Jesus, so pure and mild,
A Christmas tale, beloved child.
The Christmas story brings us near,
To love, to joy, to Christmas cheer.
So hear the story, listen close,
It's a gift of love that we all boast.
The Christmas story, sweet and bright,
A tale of peace on Christmas night.

Poem 97: "The Christmas Angels"

The Christmas angels in the sky,
With wings that sparkle, flying high.
They sing of love, they sing of peace,
A Christmas chorus that will not cease.
Their voices ring so pure and sweet,
A song of joy that can't be beat.
They spread their wings and take their flight,
A symbol of hope on Christmas night.
The angels glide through skies of blue,
They bring their blessings to me and you.
With every note, the joy they share,
A Christmas message fills the air.
The angels' song is soft and bright,
It fills our hearts with pure delight.
They remind us that love is near,
A Christmas gift that brings us cheer.
So listen close and feel the sound,
For Christmas angels all around.
Their love and peace will ever stay,
Guiding our hearts on Christmas Day.

Poem 98: "The Christmas Morning"

On Christmas morning, we awake,
With hearts so full, we can't forsake.
The joy we feel, the love we know,
It fills our hearts and starts to grow.
The stockings hang, the tree stands tall,
We gather round to share it all.
The morning sun shines bright and clear,
A day of love, a day so dear.
The presents glisten 'neath the tree,
With ribbons tied so happily.
We share our gifts, we share our cheer,
On Christmas morning, joy is near.
We laugh, we sing, we dance, we play,
For Christmas morning's here to stay.
A time of love, a time of light,
A Christmas morning pure and bright.
So rise with joy, and start your day,
For Christmas morning leads the way.
A gift of peace, a gift so sweet,
A Christmas morning, pure and neat.

Poem 99: "The Christmas Wish"

I make a wish on Christmas night,
For peace and love to take their flight.
A wish for joy, a wish for cheer,
For all the world to draw near.
I wish for kindness, I wish for grace,
To see a smile on every face.
A wish for love to spread its wings,
For peace to reign on all the things.
I wish for dreams to come alive,
For every heart to truly thrive.
A wish for joy, both big and small,
For Christmas love to fill us all.
I make a wish for Christmas cheer,
For every moment to be dear.
A wish for hope, a wish for light,
To carry us through every night.
So make your wish, so pure and true,
For Christmas dreams will come to you.
A Christmas wish, a love so bright,
Brings peace and joy on Christmas night.

Poem 100: "The Spirit of Christmas"

The spirit of Christmas fills the air,
With love and joy beyond compare.
It's in the laughter, it's in the song,
A Christmas spirit all day long.
The spirit of Christmas is in the heart,
It brings us closer, never apart.
A love that grows with every year,
A holiday joy that's always near.
The spirit of Christmas shines so bright,
It fills the world with pure delight.
It's in the kindness we give away,
A gift of love on Christmas Day.
The spirit of Christmas brings us peace,
A gift of joy that will not cease.
It lifts our hearts and lights the way,
A shining beacon every day.
So carry the spirit in your soul,
Let it guide you, make you whole.
The spirit of Christmas, pure and true,
Brings love and joy for me and you.

www.ingramcontent.com/pod-product-compliance
Ingram Content Group UK Ltd.
Pitfield, Milton Keynes, MK11 3LW, UK
UKHW041842141224
452457UK00012B/595